TIPS FOR NEW MANAGERS

BULLET GUIDE

Karen Mannering

Hodder Education, 338 Euston Road, London NW1 3BH

Hodder Education is an Hachette UK company

First published in UK 2011 by Hodder Education

This edition published 2011

Artworks (internal and cover): Peter Lubach
Cover concept design: Two Associates

British Library Cataloguing in Publication Data: a catalogue record for this title is available from the British Library.

10 9 8 7 6 5 4 3 2 1

www.hoddereducation.co.uk

Typeset by Stephen Rowling/Springworks

Printed in Spain

Contents

Acknowledgements

Thanks to Victoria Roddam and Alison Frecknall for their help and support.

About the author

Karen Mannering lives in Kent and is a specialist in people development with over 20 years' experience. She has worked in both the private and public sector and has lectured widely. Karen has a degree in Psychology and a Masters degree in Management Studies in addition to many skills-specific qualifications. She is a Fellow of the Institute of Personnel Development and a member of the British Psychological Society, the Chartered Management Institute and the Society of Women Writers and Journalists.

Karen's enthusiasm for lifelong learning and people development, together with her background in management, result in a practical but humanistic approach to introducing training into the workplace. She contributes regularly to magazines and has written many books on self-development. Her website can be found at www.karenmannering.co.uk.

Introduction

There's a plethora of management training out there, but it mainly raises two issues. The first is **timeliness**: when you become a manager you want information now, immediately – not from a course held in six months' time. The second issue is that, as a new manager, you need **practical help**. Models and theories are great, but in those first few days, when you are trying to create a presence and earn respect from the team, you are judged more by what you do than what you know.

This book aims to stop that gap with real, practical information and help, which will get you through those first weeks and create a **firm foundation** for your future.

In your first week you'll need to impress the team and, more importantly, the person who gave you the job; after all, they'll be watching to ensure that their faith in appointing you was justified. You need information NOW, and this book will tell you what you need, why you need it, and how to get it.

1 You, the manager

Getting the basics in place

You're the new manager of your own unit or team. You should feel elated, but instead you feel apprehensive, thinking:

What if there's no one there to tell me what to do?

What if I'm expected to plunge straight into the job without any help?

You know you'll be **judged** by your endeavours, and that this could be the **springboard** to a career in senior management, so it's vital to be successful.

Managing people is not easy. Even the most productive staff will be looking to you for **leadership and help**, and at the same time you'll need to be addressing the **issues and problems** of those who do not perform. It can all seem daunting, but not if you take things one step at a time. You need to start by:

* understanding the role of the manager
* being clear about whether you have the right qualities to be a manager
* the duties you will need to perform
* how to get off to a flying start.

Managing people is not easy

Why do we need managers?

Managers make things happen. They do this by:

* **planning** a way forward
* creating the **structure** that carries the plans forward
* **motivating** staff to help carry out the plans
* **evaluating** the outcome against the original plan.

This usually involves working in a continuous cycle, known as the evaluation cycle, as shown.

'The conventional definition of management is getting work done through people, but real management is developing people through work.'

Agha Hasan Abedi

What is management?

Management in business may be broadly defined as the process of using resources – which include people – effectively and efficiently in order to **accomplish desired objectives**. It's the way you go about this process that will determine your success.

Management is:

✔ process driven – a way of getting things done
✔ an opportunity to motivate staff to make things happen
✔ moving the business forward
✔ an opportunity to develop the business and the people working there.

Management is not:

✘ maintaining the status quo
✘ bullying people into doing the work you don't want to do
✘ an opportunity to sit around chatting all day
✘ one step closer to spending all day on the golf course.

The truth about managers

No matter what you may have heard about management, it is not the easiest job on earth, but it can be highly rewarding. Many people look at their own managers and think: 'If only I could move up a level. Their job looks so much easier than mine.'

However, the view is somewhat different when you get there. Managers are expected to deliver results. Therefore they may have **authority**, but that also comes with **accountability**.

Who should be a manager?

All types of people become managers, but certain personal traits may make the job of management easier.

Helpful traits and qualities	Unhelpful traits and qualities
Able to motivate, listen to and empathize with others	Does not like people
Likes to plan for the future	Prefers letting the future grow 'organically'
Likes to share work and achieve goals with others	Does not like to share
Enjoys the diversity that other people bring to work	Believes in only one way of doing things – their own
Is happy to lead a team and make decisions	Prefers to work alone

The size of your team is not important, but you'll need to find a **balance** so that, while everyone is aware that you are the manager, you are still working within the team to achieve results **TOGETHER**.

Your management duties

As a manager you have a number of duties. Since your most important resource is the people in your team, principally you have a **duty of care** to your team members. This means that you need to be aware of how the organization looks after and deals with staff, so that you can maintain or improve practices. This duty of care includes ensuring that staff:

* work in a healthy environment
* are protected from discrimination and harassment
* have opportunities for development
* are trained in the necessary tasks they have to perform
* have regular, good-quality feedback on their performance.

All organizations are required to have a **health and safety** procedure. In a small office this may be only a couple of pages long and be referred to infrequently, but in a construction company it may be a very large document (almost a book) that dictates every decision you make.

Caring for staff

Caring for staff also means looking after their development and welfare. You will need to consider all the elements of caring for staff set out in this diagram.

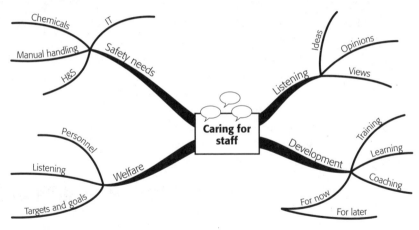

Planning your first day

Your first day as a manager can be tricky. To get off to a flying start, use the following aide-mémoire.

1 **Locate** your working area and nearby facilities.
2 **Introduce yourself** (ideally) individually to all staff, and learn their names and what they do.
3 Locate important **documents** such as the business plan, organizational chart, personnel guidance, health and safety policy and staff handbook.
4 Set up **passwords** on your computer, and find out how to maintain computer **security**.
5 Have a meeting with your **manager** to identify meetings you need to attend or decisions that have to be made in the coming week.
6 **Thank** everyone who has helped you that day.

Introduce yourself to all staff

CASE STUDY: The new manager

Chris has been appointed as a new manager at D. G. Higgins. He will have a team of five, and has been brought in to improve productivity. Chris was told at the interview that the company plans to expand, and that it may purchase two other companies in the following year.

If this happens, Chris could eventually become a senior manager. However, he first must prove himself able in this job. Chris is excited by this opportunity but knows he must start to prepare now, before he begins his first role as manager, if he is to prove his worth and move up in the company.

2 Leading the way

Leadership and management

Leadership and management are terms often used interchangeably. However, there are key differences between them. While your role as a manager is to implement company decisions and show organizational skills, you also need to be able to show that you can lead your team.

Staff will be looking to you to provide **direction** – to be their leader – as well as a **plan of action** for how to get there.

Staff will be looking to you to provide direction – to be their leader

> **'Management is doing things right, leadership is doing the right things.'**
> Peter Drucker

Leadership is just one of many qualities a successful manager must have. Whether your company calls you a manager or leader, you will be responsible for:

* providing a **vision** for your team
* integrating that vision into some form of **statement**
* creating plans and a **pathway** towards that vision
* **motivating** your team along the way.

You therefore need to be decisive and clear in your communication, so that your team feels safe in accompanying you on that journey into the future.

Why managers need to be leaders

Leadership is:

1 setting a new direction or envisioning the future
2 visualizing where you want the team to be
3 motivating staff to want to follow you
4 seeing what the team must aim to achieve.

Management is:

1 planning, organizing and directing
staff to achieve that aim
2 matching the right tasks to the
right people
3 maintaining order and control
over processes
4 problem solving.

However, the two roles are often interlocked, and both are important. For example:

Leadership without management...	Management without leadership...
...may set a direction but not tell anyone how to get there, causing chaos to ensue.	...may concentrate too much on the detail and fail to provide the 'bigger picture' for the team, in terms of where they are all supposed to be heading.

As you can see, whatever your job title, you need to be both a manager and a leader for your team. This is the way to ensure that you provide the **ultimate direction** towards their goal AND create a **realistic plan** of action for how to reach it.

Leaders also need followers, and therefore it is essential to build a team of staff who will enable you to deliver. A vision without any follow-through actions is just a dream. You want real results, and this approach embraces aspects of both management and leadership.

Having a vision

When you start your job it may be quite difficult immediately to conjure up a **vision of the future**. You may need to acclimatize yourself to the sector or do some research. To help you, ask yourself the following **questions**:

1 What is my company trying to achieve, at the highest level?
2 How does this affect me and the team (what part do we play in achieving that success)?
3 Would I like my team to grow, specialize or become more commercial?
4 Does my team (both within the organization and physically) need to move, expand or retract?

These are just some of the questions to think about to help you create that vision.

Creating a mission statement

Your vision now needs capturing in a short statement that you can use to motivate the team, give direction and include in your business plan.

This could take several forms, so look at your company's business plan and website to find out how they present their mission statement. A typical mission statement goes something like:

'Our mission is to create the best hamburger on the market by...'

(followed by a bulleted list of the ways they intend to do this).

Keep your mission statement **direct**, **short** and **snappy**.

Top tip
Don't shy away from asking your team to help you create the team mission statement. Including them in this process can help everyone bond.

Planning your way forward

Now that you have your mission statement, you should include it in your **business plan** to provide context.

Business plans are critical planning documents. Some of the reasons for creating a business plan are:

* to demonstrate how you aim to achieve your goal (or mission statement)
* to enable you to focus on how you are going to get there
* to show your boss how the work of your team will support the aims of the whole company
* to enable the team to know what they need to achieve
* to create a forecasting document for the future
* to enable you to budget effectively.

'Worry a bit now or worry a lot later.'
Jay N. Rosenblatt

Creating your business plan

Your business plan needs to detail the ideas shown in this diagram.

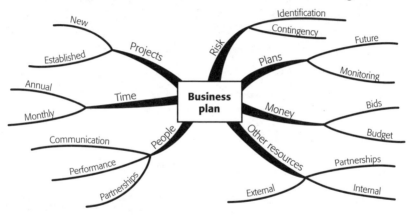

Your business plan should never reside in a drawer. It is a **living document** that should be updated with the changes in your business, and rewritten in full every year.

Motivating the team

Leaders are nothing without followers, and managers are nothing without someone to manage. It is therefore essential to spend time motivating your team to move in the same direction as your business. After all, they are going to deliver the business plan with you.

1 Start by involving all your team in writing your first business plan.
2 **Ask everyone for ideas**.
3 Check that all aspects of the team or business are included.

This will **help staff feel involved** in the new team and the formation of your new direction. Involving staff early on is also a great way of establishing yourself as leader.

Ask everyone for ideas

CASE STUDY: Meeting the team

Chris cannot find a previous business plan and so decides to create one. He makes a list of what he thinks should be included, but soon realizes that he does not really understand the extent of the work undertaken by his team. He decides to hold a meeting to involve everyone.

Chris is worried that they'll think he doesn't know enough about the work and therefore will not make a good manager – but the reverse happens. Their previous manager did not share his plans with the team, and now they are so pleased to be involved that they create lots of ideas, and thoroughly engage in helping Chris.

3 Creating a communication framework

Bringing communication into focus

There is rarely an organization that claims that its **communication** would not benefit from improvement. This aspect of business constantly needs to be brought into focus and reviewed. With so many activities going on it can be easily forgotten, and this is why it should have **special attention**.

Place it high on your agenda and you will naturally incorporate it into your business planning. It will then quickly pay dividends.

Place communication high on your agenda and it will pay dividends

> **'The single biggest problem in communication is the illusion that it has taken place.'**
>
> George Bernard Shaw

Communication is **vital** in today's workplace. To ensure you get a grip on this most important element of management, you will need to:

* identify the established forms of communication
* map out the details of your required communication lines
* create new links and analyse the range of methods you use
* build in a regular evaluation.

Team communications

A communication framework helps you to identify how much time is spent in communication and to ensure that this time is not wasted.

To produce a **communication plan**, you need to discuss what you are currently doing. Only then can you rewrite the plan and design a more **effective framework**. Use the three-ring approach to communication illustrated here to help you.

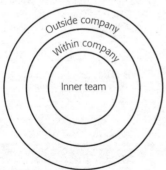

Outside company

Within company

Inner team

Top tip
Start by focusing on your team and how they communicate with each other, and extend outwards later, using the 'three-ring' process.

The communication web

Call the team together and ask them to identify everyone they communicate with within the team. They need to consider:

* all team **members** (including home or field workers)
* all **methods** (face to face, email, meetings, via mail, telephone, etc.)
* all **styles** of communication, formal (memos and letters) and informal (chatting and office banter)
* **frequency** of the communication.

Map this out so that you get a picture of the team's communication web, and question whether this is the most efficient framework.

> Communication takes two: one to relay a message and the other to receive it. If there are problems with either aspect, the outcome will not be clear.

Internal communications: the team and the organization

Once you have a pictorial representation of in-team communication, the next step is to find out how your team communicates with others outside the team.

Stay focused on the team: it's **how THE TEAM communicates** rather than the organization at large. This will demonstrate whether your team is fully integrated into all the areas of the organization, and able to access the right information for their needs.

30

Remember
It is possible to over-communicate and cause information overload. Therefore be bold in stripping out methods that are unhelpful, duplicated or unnecessary.

Answer the following questions about how your team communicates with other internal customers and staff.

- ☐ Are these communications **sufficient** to meet the team's needs?
- ☐ Are the methods used **suited** to the needs of the team?
- ☐ Would another method be more **effective**?
- ☐ Are mechanisms in place for you to **access** all team communications swiftly?

If at this stage you identify communication gaps, or areas where you are not accessing all the information you need, you'll have to identify ways of ensuring that these gaps are filled.

External communications

Finally, consider how the team communicates with the outside world.

☐ Does it have business **relationships** with staff from other companies?
☐ Does it have an **advertising** presence?
☐ Does it appear in print, broadcast or new **media** channels?
☐ **Does it sponsor** community projects?

Analyse these interactions in the same way as you did for the others.

* Are they working well for the team?
* Are there any that you need to change, modify or delete?
* Which are the most effective methods?

External communications involve sending messages about your team's vision, values and goals to stakeholders, and ensuring that these messages are understood. They depend on developing relationships and partnerships and using a variety of channels.

Creating the plan

Now that you have mapped out the three areas, and questioned the relevance of the communication in each instance, you will be able to create a plan detailing how you want your team to communicate from now on.

1 Use the **three-ring method** described earlier to provide headings.
2 Ensure that you cover **every aspect of the team's functions**.
3 **Decide** which of the communication forums or methods will remain and which will go or be replaced.
4 **Communicate your plans** both to the team and also to all other interested parties.
5 Make sure everyone understands the **changes** you and your team are making and the **reasons** for them.

'The more elaborate our means of communication, the less we communicate.'

Joseph Priestley

Building in a regular evaluation

Business moves at a tremendous pace. It could be that you and your team are constantly being asked to take on new projects or expand existing ones in new directions.

If you are operating in such a dynamic environment, it is highly unlikely that a communication plan written in January would still be suitable in May. However, it's easy to forget this unless you build into your plan a **regular point** at which evaluation will take place.

Regular evaluation of communications will enable you to make the changes needed to ensure that you always **communicate in the most appropriate way** for the business need. This will help you achieve optimum success.

Always communicate in the most appropriate way

CASE STUDY: Looking at communication

Since Chris has not found a useful communication plan, he decides to have a meeting with each team member, to discuss their communication needs in detail. He finds several areas of overlap (where rationalization could be made), a couple of gaps, and some areas where the communication method could be changed to greater effect.

Chris decides to map out his new ideas regarding communication, and builds in a two-month initial trial period. He then communicates this to the team at their Monday morning team meeting, and invites their comments. He tells everyone that they will all be involved in the evaluation in two months' time.

4 Handling the budget

Managing budgets

Budgeting is a key aspect of management. Managers are typically required to maintain an **annual budget** and present **regular forecasts** of income and expenditure. You'll need to ask yourself:

Is my mathematical ability strong enough?

Do I need help in this area?

Plenty of books and learning materials are aimed at improving your mathematical dexterity – so if you need help, don't be afraid to seek it out.

Budgeting is a key aspect of management

Depending on your business, you may be budgeting daily, monthly or quarterly. Regular **budget maintenance** allows the manager to plan ahead, keep tabs on where the money is spent or earned, and avoid the unexpected.

To maintain a budget, which is likely to be in spreadsheet format, you'll need to:

* understand the parameters of your business (what budget you have been given, where it is typically spent, etc.)
* explore the mechanisms in your workplace for processing money
* start to plan out your proposed expenditure and income
* stay on top of your figures and report as necessary.

Analysing your budget

When you first find yourself in the position of manager, **identify your budget** as soon as possible. You'll need to:

1 access any previous budgets (to gauge past performance)
2 look through the headings to see what details are collected (you should be able to search on these later)
3 ask for clarification of headings you are unsure of.

40

Top tip
It's far better to ask for clarification at this stage than make a mistake later.

What to look for

In your budget, **look at each heading** to see where the money is spent.
Ask yourself the following questions:

- ☐ Do I have to pay for salaries or consultancy fees (which can reduce the budget dramatically)?
- ☐ Has there been significant one-off expenditure (such as refitting an office) that I would not have to pay for again?
- ☐ Are there investments that (possibly) could be drawn on later?
- ☐ Am I carrying previous investment (i.e. payments that have to be honoured)?
- ☐ Are there any seasonal differences?

'Annual income twenty pounds, annual expenditure nineteen and six, result happiness. Annual income twenty pounds, annual expenditure twenty pound ought and six, result misery.'

Charles Dickens

Budgets in the workplace

From a managerial perspective, you need to find out how money flows in the workplace. For example, if you contract with an outside body to do work for you:

* Is that allowed (are you allowed to purchase direct or do you need managerial permission)?
* How (and to whom) do they address their invoices?
* How soon will they be paid?

Most organizations have a specific way of purchasing goods and services and settling payment. For example, you may have to raise a **purchase order** before buying, and local government organizations may have a **preferred supplier list** from which you must select your provider.

Top tip
Ask your company accountant or another manager for advice on budgets.

Cost codes

Larger organizations and companies that undertake project work often use cost codes against which you place your expenditure. This allows finance personnel to:

* keep a **running account of each area** of the business or project
* draw off **reports** of spending and income on each project, providing senior managers (or the company board) with an **overview of spending** and progression.

If you're unsure about this, ask your financial officer. He or she will also be the person who allocates you codes for the projects under your control.

Top tip
Record your cost codes in a book or pin them up so that you have them to hand – you'll need them regularly!

Find out how money flows in the workplace

Planning the budget

Each year you'll be expected to plan your budget for the year ahead. This will need to take into account:

* **ongoing expenditure** (including long-term commitments)
* projected **new spend**.

1 Look back at previous budgets to see what's required and which factors to include. In addition to your own costs you'll need to include your team in predicting future spend, as they will have a view on their own area.
2 If you need to ask for an increase in budget, expect to be asked to present a solid business case for requesting more money.
3 Always build in a **contingency** plan of **at least 10 per cent** in case things go wrong (or prices rise).

Budget maintenance

Now you have your budget, you'll need to maintain it.

* **Ask your finance officer** or accountant how they'd like your budgets managed. They'll probably ask you to use the program they use so that all data can be read electronically.
* Put time aside for a **weekly budget check**. By keeping your finger on the pulse, you'll see problems as they arise rather than finding out about them later.
* Regular budget maintenance will **save time** at the point of consolidation.

> Budgets don't have to be managed by computer, but it makes things easier: you can draw on a range of data – such as all contractor costs over several months – in just a few keystrokes.

The budget cycle

Every organization fits its budget into its own **business cycle**. This means that the budgetary cycle does not necessarily mirror the calendar year or even the tax year.

If you are unsure, find out now so that you know when to complete and present your budget returns. (Finding out that you have £100,000 left in the budget, and only one month left in which to spend it, places you in a very different position from discovering that you have the same amount but ten months left.)

Once you have been through one budgetary cycle, you'll gain a more measured insight into how the budget should run, including seasonal highs and lows.

> **Remember**
> Make sure you give enough time to the task of your weekly budget review, so that you can immediately see when your spending is going adrift.

CASE STUDY: Looking at the budget

Chris hasn't managed a budget before but feels that his school maths will be sufficient to get by. He asks his manager to talk him through the current budget.

He notices that items are coded and is told he must stick to these codes. He also notices figures in euros: the company deals with a French supplier, so he must convert currency to build that cost into his budget. Chris asks for an IT program to deal with the conversion.

Chris decides to share the budget with the team and have it on the agenda at each weekly team meeting. He also decides that it would be good practice for one member of the team to learn how to run the budget in case he's ever away.

5 Delegating with success

Effective delegation

You will need to delegate tasks in your role as a manager. Delegating effectively is not the same as sharing out your work portfolio, and then sitting back. You should only delegate tasks when:

* your **workload** is too great
* another member of the team has more **experience** in that topic than you
* a member of your team would **benefit** from the development offered by undertaking that project.

When you delegate tasks you still maintain overall responsibility

> **'Never tell people how to do things.**
> **Tell them what to do and they will**
> **surprise you with their ingenuity.'**
>
> General George Smith Patton Jr

It's crucial that when you delegate tasks you still maintain **overall responsibility** for ensuring that the task is completed successfully and within the correct time frame.

The process of **delegation** involves:

* identifying **topics** for delegation
* deciding on the **right person** to do the task
* **monitoring** and giving feedback
* **evaluating** the success of the delegation.

What to delegate

Delegating suitable tasks or topics can free up a manager's time, while also giving staff valuable work experience that can aid their development. It also provides a **'safety net'** for times when you are unavailable.

Not all work is suitable for delegation. For example:

Good-quality delegated tasks	Poor-quality delegated tasks
Taking over the daily running of the team budget	Asking someone to attend the odd meeting whenever you can't make it
Writing a report	Complex customer negotiations

The poor-quality tasks are not distinct enough, and if the team member took on these types of task only intermittently, it would be hard to measure their impact. A good-quality delegated task should have methods of monitoring and evaluation built in so that, as a manager, you can assess not only the performance of the other person but also how successful the delegation has been.

Whether you work in an office or a factory, look at the work you do in terms of **distinct topics or projects**. Now make a list of the topics or projects that could be delegated. Topics suitable for delegation must be:

1 **whole projects** in themselves (not odd tasks)
2 **timebound,** with distinct start and end dates
3 **stretching,** containing some form of learning for the team member
4 **achievable** and realistic.

Choosing the right recipient

You have your list of topics and now you need to think broadly about your team and who might be possible candidates to take them on. You need to consider:

* their current **workload** – you must be aware of overloading staff
* their **qualifications and experience** – some staff may have more expertise than you in certain subjects
* the **reason** for the delegation:
  » Is your aim to develop staff? (This may take a little longer if they need support or training to achieve the task.)
  » Is your aim to get the task done quickly? (This implies that you need someone with a proven track record of performing well in that area.)

Allocation of tasks or projects must be transparent

Allocation of tasks or projects must be **transparent** and handled with **equity** in mind. The best way to do this is during a team meeting with everyone present.

Do:
- ✔ explain to everyone what the project is and why it is being delegated
- ✔ ask for volunteers
- ✔ identify someone if you think they are the most suitable person – and explain why
- ✔ ensure that everyone takes a task and that equity is uppermost.

Don't:
- ✘ try to hide what you are doing
- ✘ allocate projects without consultation
- ✘ overload the most talented person in the team
- ✘ show favouritism by giving the best projects to people you like.

Monitoring progress

In delegating work you are not delegating all accountability. It's essential to provide support at the beginning and maintain close contact throughout the project.

Initially, staff need **good-quality communication** from you to outline the project and their part in its success. They'll need to know:

* what's required (what part they play)
* what background information they need
* who the main players are (and any other contacts or partnerships)
* the parameters (budget, time, resources)
* how the project will be monitored and measured.

Throughout the project you will need to build in regular meetings to ensure progress, and to discuss any difficulties along the way.

* Offer **coaching** to team members working on a delegated task. You are ultimately responsible for the outcome of the delegation, and so you must be in overall control.
* Offer any necessary training programmes to support staff in the delegation. It will be an investment for the future.
* Give regular **feedback** on the task or project so that they know how you view their progress.
* Give personal feedback regarding how the person has coped and what they have learned.

Giving personal feedback
Personal feedback should:
* concentrate on the positive outcomes of the project/task
* address any problems
* finish with an action plan demonstrating a way forward.

Evaluating the success of the delegation

At the end of the delegation period it's helpful to undertake an evaluation so that you can ascertain both the success of the delegation and what has been learned from it.

Success can be measured in a number of ways:

☐ Was the task completed within the allotted **time**?
☐ Did it come in on **budget**?
☐ Was the customer happy with the **outcome**?
☐ Has the staff member learned or developed **new skills**?
☐ Could they **undertake** that delegated task again with a high level of confidence?

All of these are valuable measures, but the relevance and importance of each one will depend on how you view a successful outcome.

CASE STUDY: Delegating

Chris knows he'll have to delegate projects if he is to deliver on his own job. Although he's shaping up as a manager, he knows he's not always the most appropriate person for certain tasks. However, he has experience of work being dumped on him, and he's anxious not to do this to his staff.

He holds a team meeting to discuss the projects and ask for volunteers. By asking people to choose the projects they'd like to take on, he keeps the process transparent and finds no need for coercion: for some, the projects play to their strengths, and for others they represent development opportunities. Chris starts to feel positive about the future as he recognizes the versatility within his team.

6 Developing the team

Effective staff development

Your team is like a living organism and needs nourishing if it is to flourish. This nourishing takes the form of staff development. Effective staff and team development:

* supports people's needs
* supports the projects undertaken by the team
* provides new skills
* is motivating and enriching.

A good employer also strives to **maximize the potential** of every member of staff for the benefit of the whole organization.

Your team needs nourishing if it is to flourish

Staff and team development adds significantly to the **effectiveness** of people and increases **job satisfaction**, which in turn improves **staff retention**.

Your individual staff members and the team as a whole both need development. It helps to think of them as two distinctly different developmental areas. However, to consider every angle you need to:

* undertake a **skills analysis** for each team member
* map this analysis against the **needs** of the team
* decide on suitable **interventions** to provide new skills
* **incorporate** the **learning** and skills into your overall strategy.

Undertaking a skills analysis

The components of any job break down into three areas:

1 **skills** (what we can do)
2 **knowledge** (what we know)
3 **performance** (how we apply these to our job).

There could be deficiencies in any of these areas, both for individuals and the team. Your role is to uncover the skills gaps by undertaking a skills analysis.

You'll also need to know whether any of your team are working towards professional qualifications, and factor these in.

'You can teach a student a lesson for a day; but if you can teach him to learn by creating curiosity, he will continue the learning process as long as he lives.'

Clay P. Bedgord

Individual analysis

Since your analysis is to cover both individual needs and the collective team, start by holding individual meetings with all staff to find out where they feel they need development to help them in their jobs. You can also use **job descriptions** to find out how staff skills, knowledge and performance match up to their jobs and responsibilities.

Team analysis

Team analysis is best undertaken with the whole team, perhaps during a team meeting. It is not unusual for staff to be individually highly qualified but not function effectively as a team. Teams perform best when everyone is **pulling together** in the same direction.

Training needs can be of three types:
1 those you can anticipate
2 those that arise from monitoring
3 those arising from unforeseen problems.

They may be at the organization level as well as at the team or individual level.

Mapping skills against needs

Once you understand everyone's strengths and areas for development, you need to map them against not just the current workload but also that of the future.

As a manager setting the **strategy** for your team, you are in the privileged position of knowing the direction in which the business will move. This means that you can organize **suitable programmes** of staff development before the critical time when the skills are needed.

66

By **analysing the tasks** to be performed and the **requirements** for performing them, you can specify the **skills** required. This will ensure that any training or development is relevant to the content of the job.

Mapping development needs will help you:	Mapping development needs will not help you:
✔ *plan for the future*	✘ *provide for every eventuality*
✔ *allocate the correct amount of money for development*	✘ *pay for everything you want to achieve*
✔ *motivate staff.*	✘ *keep staff who really want to leave.*

Remember
If the skills or knowledge incorporate a qualification or similar form of prolonged learning, they may take a long time to acquire, and therefore this must be built into your future plans.

Suitable interventions

When we think of staff development we often think of **training** programmes, but this is not the only method of development. How about:

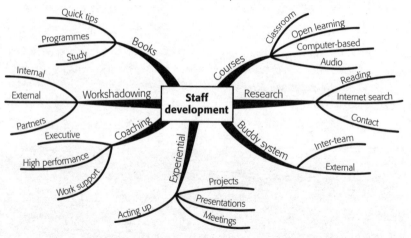

The intervention you select needs to strike a **balance** between your staff's preferred **style of learning** and the **logistics** of incorporating that into your workplace.

If you do decide to select a traditional training programme, make sure that you understand and agree the content. The number of candidates you have will also influence whether you would send your staff to an advertised course, or arrange an in-house programme.

A public course is:

* generic by nature, and therefore you may not be able to influence the content
* only cheaper if you send just one or two people
* a forum where people from different organizations can interact.

An in-house programme is:

* tailored by you, so you have total control over the content
* good for staff dynamics, since you are likely to need at least six people to create a group
* usually cheaper for several people.

Incorporating learning into your strategy

Skills development is investment in people who will ultimately deliver your projects. Once you've decided on your staff development plan, you'll have details of:

* **where** skills in the team lie
* **who** needs additional development
* **how** the development will take place.

All these details need summarizing and including in your strategy and business plan. There is a cost to staff development, which must be factored into your team budget and timescale.

CASE STUDY: Developing staff

Chris decides to take a two-pronged approach and look at the team separately from its members. He meets everyone individually to find out their skills and where they feel they need development. He also decides that the team needs some facilitated group time to bond together more fully and improve their communication.

Chris has two team members needing project management skills, and so he opts to send them on a programme with a local company. Before booking, he checks the course outline to make sure it meets their needs. Before bringing in a facilitator to work with the whole team, he consults HR and several managers, and then speaks to two professional facilitators before engaging one.

7 Dealing with poor performance

Managing performance issues

In an ideal world your team would always work productively, leaving you free to concentrate on planning, monitoring and strategy. However, management means facing the possibility that at some point some staff will – for a variety of reasons – perform at a lower than acceptable standard.

This problem is not that unusual, and therefore knowing how to handle poor performance while **staying within the law** is immensely useful.

'Electric communication will never be a substitute for the face of someone who with their soul encourages another person to be brave and true.'

Charles Dickens

Talk to an HR professional at the earliest point

Dealing with **performance issues** can get out of hand, so talk to an HR professional at the earliest point. This is especially important if the situation escalates, as every step you take will be critical. With this in mind, be aware of:

* what constitutes poor performance
* communicating acceptable behaviour
* creating an action plan
* measuring poor performance.

What is poor performance?

We tend to know when someone is **underperforming**, but we're often unsure about when to step in and what to do.

Start by analysing what poor performance might look like. It could be:

☐ coming in late or leaving early
☐ unexplained absences
☐ taking an excessive amount of time off
☐ missing deadlines
☐ failing to meet objectives

…or any other situation where you feel performance does not meet the company's expectations.

Effects on the team

You may find yourself reluctant to intervene, but allowing poor performance to continue unchecked has **dire effects** on the team. For example, other team members may:

* work to alienate the underperformer, fragmenting the team
* consider you, the manager, to be weak for not dealing with the situation
* feel resentment, since poor performance usually means that everyone else has to do more to carry the load of the team
* reduce their own performance if they see someone apparently getting away with doing less.

All these factors make for **uncomfortable team dynamics**, making it a team problem as well as an individual one.

'It is an immutable law in business that...promises are promises but only performance is reality.'

Harold S. Geneen

Communicating team objectives

Staff can't be expected to know what is required of them unless they are told. It is for this reason that you need to **set firm objectives** and communicate them to everyone. These objectives need to cover:

1 **work activity** (WHAT each team member does)
2 **behaviour** (HOW each team member operates).

Discuss them with the team, so that everyone is aware of working to the same standards and expectations. However, discuss personal performance against these outcomes **privately,** in one-to-one meetings.

> Poor performance often reflects how effectively an organization is led. It may result from role overload, unclear objectives or unrealistic targets. Always address these issues first in cases of poor performance.

78

Setting individual objectives

Setting individual objectives for everyone provides a way of stating each person's work expectations. Objectives need to be written in a way that enables them to be easily monitored. Write them in **SMART** format to ensure they contain all the factors required for creating solid, measurable objectives. SMART is a mnemonic standing for:

Note
Objectives should contain all these aspects.

- ☐ **S** – specific: no ambiguity
- ☐ **M** – measurable: this could be in time, cost, or quality
- ☐ **A** – agreed with the team: to ensure their understanding
- ☐ **R** – realistic: can this actually be achieved?
- ☐ **T** – time span: there needs to be a time frame for achievement.

Giving feedback and action planning

Hold **one-to-one meetings** with all staff to assess their performance on a regular basis. Making this a regular feature in the diary reduces the fear factor for staff, and these meetings will very much become 'the way we do things around here'.

This meeting offers you an ideal opportunity to discuss projects and behaviour, and quickly address any issues or concerns. Problems addressed quickly are much easier to sort out before they escalate, and **regular meetings** provide that opportunity to talk about problems at an early stage.

Top tip
Encourage open communication during these meetings, but keep the focus firmly fixed on work matters.

It's vital to **record** every meeting. Keeping notes of your discussion (signed and dated by both of you) ensures that you have an official record of what's been discussed and agreed.

At the end of each meeting, set out an action plan to take both of you forward. **Action planning** is a positive way of continuing the discussion into the next meeting.

* **For staff performing well**, an action plan offers a structured way forwards.
* **For staff performing less well,** it allows you to set new targets for improving behaviour or completing projects. This sends a powerful message to the individual that you're happy to keep them in the team if they improve.

Quickly address any issues or concerns

Measuring poor performance

If you have written and **agreed objectives** for all your team, measuring performance against those measures should be fairly simple. Improvement targets should also be written in SMART format.

It is crucial to record every aspect of staff performance, to provide **evidence** for any future pay award or bonus – or job termination.

Unfortunately, not everyone steps up to meet those plans, and if you decide that the only option for the team is to part company, always speak to an HR professional before taking action. If your company does not have an HR unit or expert, contact a local business organization, such as your Chamber of Commerce, for advice.

Remember
An employer wishing to dismiss a member of staff must follow strict disciplinary procedures. Failure to follow these could have serious and costly repercussions for the business.

CASE STUDY: Addressing poor performance

Chris has noticed that one team member, Paula, is performing less well than the others. Since the weekly team meeting is not the appropriate place to tackle this issue, he decides to introduce monthly one-to-one meetings.

The team is sceptical, but he assures everyone that this will allow him to find out how everyone performs individually. Chris lets them think up a witty name for the meetings (to help with ownership) and books time with everyone.

At Paula's one-to-one she opens up to Chris, telling him about problems with one of her projects that she didn't want to mention in the full meeting. Chris is able to offer her advice, and they adjust her targets to accommodate the delay caused by these problems.

8 Managing your stress levels

Dealing with pressure

When you take on a new job, there's always a 'honeymoon period' when everything new and interesting seems exciting. Every **challenge** is the start of new learning, and you feel able to rise to meet it head on.

However, later on, when the challenges are coming thick and fast, you may start to feel drained. Where has your enthusiasm gone, and how can you get it back?

Managing people comes with its own pressures

> **'The time to relax is when you don't have time for it.'**
> Sydney J. Harris

The first thing you need to recognize is that managing people comes with its own pressures, in addition to those presented by the actual work. However, like so many things, **anticipating** this now, in advance of those pressures, will help you get a head start. You need to:

* **be real** about your situation
* kick your **time management** into place
* build a group of **support** contacts
* **deal with the stress** as soon as it starts to build.

Being real

While some stress is normal in life, excessive stress interferes with your productivity and reduces your physical and emotional health, so it's important to find ways to keep it under control.

Where are the **stressors** likely to be in your job? They might include:

* the **people** in your team
* your own **manager**
* time constraints and **deadlines**
* **learning** new information
* **budget** constraints
* taking **risks**
* lack of project **control**

and there may be many more. Fortunately, there are ways to reduce work stress, including:

1 **taking responsibility** for your physical and emotional well-being
2 identifying **habits and negative attitudes** that add to your work stress
3 learning **better communication skills** to improve your workplace relationships.

Make your own list of things you think might cause you stress over the next three months. This is not about being negative – it's about being **REAL**.

Face your demons and you have a good chance of fighting them off; pretend they are not there and you'll not be ready for them. **Anticipate stressors** and you can plan and put actions in place; ignore them and you'll be caught unawares.

Time management

Your organization is buying your **time** and **expertise**, and they will want to be assured that you are able to **deliver** on both scores. If you find yourself:

* missing meetings
* arriving at places without the correct paperwork
* cancelling staff meetings because work is more important
* having to stay late every night (rather than choosing to)
* forgetting to do certain actions
* relying on luck or other people to carry you through

…and if your diary looks out of control, reconsider your time management.

> For in-depth information on time management, see the reading list at the end of this book, or go on a course.

* Time management techniques only work if you **put them into action**. We may know what to do, but feel too busy to start or too comfortable with our current way of working.
* Sometimes we must all **step out of our comfort zone** and invest time to learn and practise something new, to reap the benefits in the long term.
* **Look at your time management NOW** – not when work overwhelms you.

Ask yourself the following questions:

Where can I make economies?
Can I double up meetings?
Would delegating help?

Support at work

Find out if you have access to professional support at work (perhaps through a **counselling** service). If not, think about colleagues with whom you can speak confidentially. Talking can help reduce stress.

If your problem is specific, perhaps a workplace **coach** could help you. Using someone in your workplace has benefits, but you also need to be aware of the possible drawbacks.

Benefits	Drawbacks
They will know your situation and the key players.	They may have ulterior motives.
They are 'on tap' whenever you need them.	You may see them regularly in other meetings – and they will know your weaknesses.
They may be able to make practical suggestions about your work.	They could set you up or give you bad advice.

Support outside work

You may feel more comfortable with **personal support** from outside the workplace. However, there are benefits and pitfalls to be aware of here too.

Benefits	Drawbacks
The conversation is totally private.	They won't know your exact situation or the people and their personalities.
You can stop the conversation at any point with no hard feelings.	Their responses or advice may be out of context and inappropriate to the situation.
Their responses can be 'outside the box' because they can think freely.	If you are just moaning to a friend, that might be quite a test of friendship.

Remember
Sport and other outside activities such as voluntary work are also great destressors.

Recognize it – deal with it!

Don't wait for stress to creep up on you. If you see a heavy workload ahead, put in place an **action plan** for dealing with it. Our stress level depends on how much we feel in control of a situation.

* If we feel **out of control**, we will feel stressed and overwhelmed.
* If we feel **in control**, we may have a lot to do, but psychologically we have order and a plan for achieving it.

94

Snatch control back by **creating a plan** NOW. Your plan should include:

* sensible eating
* regular exercise
* involving your team in drawing up work methods that may include:
    » delegation of tasks
    » different ways of working.

Don't wait for stress to creep up on you

CASE STUDY: Action planning

Chris knows September will be a difficult month. An internal assessment will coincide with the submission by all managers of their business plans and financial forecasts for the year. In addition, the project to replace the computers is running late, and they now want to do the changeover in September.

Chris asks his team to take an hour every day to tidy the files ready for assessment. He suggests a weekly item of finance and business planning on the team agenda, so that they will only need to do minor 'tweaking' at the last minute. He tells the IT manager that the computers must be changed at another time.

By gaining control of the situation, Chris feels better, and the team is pleased to have such a firm leader.

9 Building the team

Creating a dynamic team

By now you are settling into your role. You've set up team meetings and individual meetings with all staff. You've assigned work and put performance measures in place, and you've looked at your own ways of working.

Everything is ticking along at base level, and now it's time to consider how to stretch everyone further, to create a dynamic team that not only **gets things done** but also **raises your profile**.

It's time to stretch everyone further, to create a dynamic team

> **'It is amazing how much you can accomplish when it doesn't matter who gets the credit.'**
>
> Unknown

Many people think **team building** is something to consider only when there are problems, but this is not so. As mentioned earlier, team building needs to be on your agenda from the beginning. You need to consider:

* what type of team you want
* how to share skills and expertise
* the benefits of holding a team event
* ways to move the team forward.

Your **team structure** and the way everyone operates and interacts need to produce the results you are expected to deliver.

What kind of team do you want?

Every team is different in the way its members interact. In some, members rarely meet, while in others they socialize. Some of this behaviour comes from the individuals themselves, but the most influence should come from you, as the manager or team leader.

As a manager and leader, you have a significant impact on the way a team forms and operates, so you'll need to know what sort of team you want. What type of team would be the **most effective for your business**? If the team you have doesn't produce the best outcomes as it stands, you'll need to think again.

What type of team would be the most effective?

Without firm direction, teams will develop organically and may or may not end up as **fit for purpose**. You may have been brought in to place a structure throughout an unstructured team, or even as a manager of two merging teams. If either of these is the case, you'll have to go back to the drawing board.

> **Top tip**
> If you've inherited a team, don't simply accept the status quo.

You may even be looking at a **complete restructure** of the team, including all the nuances. This restructuring may cause initial disruption, but your emerging 'new' team will then be designed specifically for the greatest impact and effect.

Every team is different in the way its members interact

Sharing skills and expertise

One area you need to consider is whether you want (or need) a
multiskilled team, where everyone can cover each other's jobs, or one
where each team member has a **distinct area of expertise**. There are
benefits to both approaches.

Benefits of a multiskilled team	Benefits of a team comprising individual skills
If anyone is off sick someone else can cover.	There are specialists in each area.
The job can be made more interesting, and staff can teach each other.	Each specialist can concentrate on their distinct area and knows it thoroughly.
There is always more to learn, so less boredom.	Staff feel more pride in knowing one subject thoroughly.

Whichever overall approach works best for your team, you may like to consider a **two-stage structure**. This is where you have some key skills or work activities that everyone can do, and then additional specialists. Structuring the team in this way gives the following benefits:

✔ greater *flexibility* on everyday tasks
✔ more staff *interaction*, where duties are shared
✔ a level of *specialism* in the subject areas that need depth of knowledge
✔ a *reduced level of risk* if someone is away from work for a time.

Holding a team event

A team event can seal the new team structure, and may last from a couple of hours to a few days, depending on your agenda.

Key questions to ask yourself

1 What am I trying to achieve?
2 What should the tone be (fun, serious, direct or visionary)?
3 What is my ultimate objective?
4 Will this event foster rapport and raise morale?
5 Will it fit into the organization's strategy?
6 Are there any staff with a disability?

Key questions to ask the team

1 Have you had team events before?
2 If so, what were they and how were they received?
3 What types of event does the company support?
4 Given what I would like to achieve, what would the team like to suggest?
5 Is there anything I need to know to ensure inclusion?

104

Designing your team event

Whether you run your own event or bring in a facilitator, you must have clear objectives and some idea of your desired outcome.

The benefit of designing and running your own team day	The benefit of bringing in help
You are in control and can switch and change subject if need be. (If you are inexperienced, this may seem daunting.)	You become one of the team and you can enter the discussions without worrying about what comes next or trying to write everything down.

Remember
If you use a facilitator, you are delegating the **task**, not the **responsibility** – so you need to approve the outline, content and expected outcomes in advance.

Moving the team forward

The final section of a team development session is usually a return to the action points arising from the session. In other words, what's everyone going to do to make them happen? And who'll do what?

If hours are spent discussing issues, only for the team to disperse, nothing changes. If nothing changes as a result of four or more people spending hours together, the event has been a waste of time and money. You can prevent this by following these four steps.

1 Draw up an **action list**.
2 Ask for a **volunteer** to take each point forward.
3 Make it clear that you'll **monitor progress** through your one-to-one meetings.
4 Say that actions completed will start the next development session.

This way the team development session becomes part of a continuous improvement cycle.

CASE STUDY: Holding a team away day

Chris's team hasn't experienced a team day before, but they've heard that they often include fun events like paintballing. They are surprised when Chris books a meeting room in a nearby hotel to discuss his ideas.

Chris produces an agenda complete with the outcomes he wants to achieve. It looks like hard work – not at all what they expected! However, they achieve a great deal and make a list of action points. Chris sets another date six months ahead for a follow-up.

Later, Brenda tells Chris that she's glad the team day was not something physical (like paintballing) because she has a bad back. Chris is pleased that he chose a non-vigorous event in which everyone could participate.

10 Your future career in management

Your future career

Becoming a manager can open up whole new career lines that you may not have considered. Being in management is not a destination but a journey. Your career could take off in many different ways, so think about the possible **opportunities**.

Much of this book has discussed how you interact and manage others, but how do you handle your own **development**? It's great to support others, but who's supporting you?

Being in management is not a destination but a journey
• •

Management has its own **career structure**, with increasingly complex issues to keep you busy. The range is vast, from managing a packing line in a factory, for example, to managing hospitality staff for the Olympics – very different in size, complexity, budget, longevity and impact.

Now that you are a manager, the expectation is that you will remain in some form of management. You therefore need to think about how you can expand your knowledge by:

* increasing your **experience**
* gaining management **qualifications**
* joining a **professional** body
* working towards **promotion**.

Increasing your experience

Being a manager means that you can undertake **complex projects**, **deliver** within constraints, and **motivate** staff sufficiently to obtain results. These are great skills upon which to build.

Before starting this job you probably imagined what being a manager entailed, and that seemed challenge enough. Once in the job, you discovered that the reality was different, but you are caught up in learning the basics and too busy to look ahead.

Some managers stop at this point: because they are so busy, they don't pay attention to their own career. When their unit closes down, they haven't looked outside their 'bubble' of experience, and have little to offer another employer.

Don't be caught in this situation. Keep learning and gaining experience, and opportunities will open up for you.

1 Think about the **type of management** you are engaged in. Would other businesses use managers with your experience? Find out, and record your thoughts so you don't forget them.
2 If you are interested in **another business area**, use your contacts to speak with a manager there – their comments could be revealing.
3 Find a manager with a **more complex team** than yours and ask to workshadow them. You'll gain valuable insight into the job, and you can 'test the waters' before moving.

Project management is an area that also offers many opportunities.

'The worst days of those who enjoy what they do are better than the best days of those who don't.'

E. James Rohn

Management qualifications

Experience is only half the story: the other half is qualifications. Qualifications add kudos to your experience, and the two together will offer any employer an attractive package.

Qualifications represent **what you know**, and some also demonstrate that you have applied certain models to your workplace. Although they don't take the place of practical experience, they do provide the learner with the background to **key management concepts**.

Qualifications add kudos to your experience

Having a management qualification is a great way of demonstrating to employers and your team that you are a **professional** manager possessing high levels of management skills. However, it can be difficult to decide what qualification to choose, since there are many different options.

For more information and for a list of management qualifications and programmes available in your area, contact:

* your local college
* your nearest university
* any business school
* adult education departments.

For advice, speak with the institute that governs your professional area, or contact the **Chartered Management Institute** (details in the What next? section at the back of this book).

Joining a professional body

There are professional bodies that cover the industry you are in (such as pharmaceuticals) or the level of your profession (management). Joining a professional body will **increase your reputation** as a manager, and you will be taken far more seriously. It will also offer you a number of services, including:

* **links** to other people in your industry or profession
* **advice** in various formats, including legal advice
* the opportunity to either join or start a **local group**
* regular **information** (website and journal)
* up-to-date **news** on government initiatives and changes in the law.

Not everyone is eligible to join a professional body, and therefore it is worth checking admittance guidelines before applying.

Many professional bodies admit members at a number of levels, ranging from Associate to Fellow, to denote experience or seniority. Join at whatever level you can. This will give you access to all their periodicals, information, meetings and library. Once you have been accepted you can work towards the higher levels.

From time to time professional bodies also offer **development opportunities**. They might need:

* a group to research a certain topic
* someone to run an evaluation
* a person to construct a feature for their magazine
* someone to write a set of standards.

This could help you broaden your experience and **enhance your CV** without having to change jobs.

Working towards promotion

The next step for you will be to look towards promotion. Promotion is not just the next level up in terms of management: it could also mean taking on a larger team, a team with complex budget problems, or a team that is failing. Ask yourself the following questions.

☐ Am I **happy** in my current business sector?
☐ What **challenges** would I be looking for in my next management job?
☐ What **opportunities** exist in my current workplace?
☐ What opportunities exist outside my workplace?
☐ What do I need to add to my skills and experience to provide **evidence** that I can perform at the next level?

'The secret of success is constancy to purpose.'
Benjamin Disraeli

118

CASE STUDY: Moving on

Chris recognizes that he has his hands full with the team, and wants to see them through to success before thinking of moving on. However, he knows that in order to move onwards and upwards he needs to gain more experience and some qualifications.

To start with, Chris signs up to do two one-day programmes that are being offered in-house. These will help him with a number of immediate issues. He then hopes to join an institute and, in time, undertake a diploma at the local college. He's already started to plan his future, and can see that management is a profession in its own right that can take him places.

What next?

This book has given you some tools and techniques to help you in your first months as a new manager, focusing on setting up processes for business and organizing your team. Due to the broad nature of management, your role will encompass many other factors over the longer term, and you can continue your learning by reading the books and accessing the websites listed below:

Allen, David, *Getting Things Done: How to Achieve Stress-free Productivity* (London: Piatkus, 2002)

Cook, Helen, and Tate, Karen, *The McGraw-Hill 36-Hour Project Management Course* (New York: McGraw-Hill Professional, 2005)

Mannering, Karen, *Negotiating: Bullet Guide* (London: Hodder Education, 2011)

The Project Management Institute at www.pmi.org offers internationally recognized qualifications for project managers.

The Chartered Management Institute at www.managers.org.uk has a good range of articles and management training courses.

The International Management Institute at www.imi.edu offers several management development programmes.